The Magic Pot

David Calcutt

Illustrated by Rebecca Gryspeerdt

OXFORD
UNIVERSITY PRESS

OXFORD

UNIVERSITY PRESS

Great Clarendon Street, Oxford OX2 6DP

Oxford University Press is a department of the University of Oxford.
It furthers the University's objective of excellence in research, scholarship,
and education by publishing worldwide in

Oxford New York

Auckland Cape Town Dar es Salaam Hong Kong Karachi
Kuala Lumpur Madrid Melbourne Mexico City Nairobi
New Delhi Shanghai Taipei Toronto

With offices in

Argentina Austria Brazil Chile Czech Republic France Greece
Guatemala Hungary Italy Japan Poland Portugal Singapore South
Korea Switzerland Thailand Turkey Ukraine Vietnam

British Library Cataloguing in Publication Data

Data available
ISBN-13: 978 0 19 915938 3
ISBN-10: 019 915938 6
10 9 8 7 6 5 4 3 2

Also available in packs
Years 3–4 Playscripts Mixed Pack (one of each playscript) ISBN 0 19 917898 4
Years 3–4 Playscripts Guided Reading Pack The Magic Pot (six copies) ISBN 0 19 915944 0

Design by Sue Clarke

Printed in Hong Kong

Cast list

(in order of appearance)

 **Villager 1** } *who tell parts of the story*
Villager 2 } *to the audience*

 **Poor Man** *who has no food or money*

 **Rich Man** *the head man of the village*

 **Wife** *married to the poor man*

 **Durga** *a great goddess who knows everything*

 **Gossip** *who likes to spread gossip around the village*

 **Daughter** *of the rich man*

 **Husband** *married to the rich man's daughter*

 **Demon** *a horrible creature carrying a club*

Scene 1

*Two **Villagers** enter and speak to the audience.*

Villager 1 Listen to our story.

Villager 2 It's a story from our village–

Villager 1 Our village in India.

Villager 2 And in our village there once lived a poor man–

*The **Poor Man** enters and stands on one side of the stage.*

Villager 1 And a rich man–

*The **Rich Man** enters and stands on the other side of the stage.*

Poor Man The poor man was very poor.

Rich Man And the rich man was very rich.

Villager 2 And they both lived in this same village–

Villager 1   Our village–

Villager 2   That stood at the edge of a great forest.

Villager 1   Now, this poor man was so poor, that he and his family had nothing to eat.

Villager 2   So, one day his wife said to him:

*The poor man's **Wife** enters and speaks to him.*

Wife   Husband. You'd better go to the head man of our village. Ask him for help.

Poor Man   Why should he help us?

Wife   He's the head man, isn't he? It's his duty to help us. Go to him and ask him for help.

*The **Poor Man** walks across to the **Rich Man** as the **Villagers** speak.*

Villager 1   So he went to the head man–

Villager 2   Who was also the rich man.

Villager 1 He had more goats than anyone else.

Villager 2 He had more cattle than anyone else.

Villager 1 He owned more land than anyone else.

Villager 2 He had more food than anyone else.

Villager 1 He had more than enough to spare.

Villager 2 He had more than enough to share.

Villager 1 He could have easily given something to the poor man.

Villager 2 But he didn't.

*The **Rich Man** speaks angrily to the **Poor Man**.*

Rich Man   How dare you come here begging! Why should I give you anything? This is my land. These are my cattle. These are my chickens and goats and sheep. I worked for them all and they're mine. There are no beggars in my village. Go away, or I'll have you thrown out!

*The **Rich Man** goes.*

Villager 1   So the poor man went back to his wife–

Villager 2   And he told her what the rich man had said–

Poor Man   And she said to him:

Wife   If he won't help us, perhaps the gods will. Go to the forest and pray to them. Most of all, pray to Durga, the great goddess.

Poor Man   Are you mad? The gods won't listen to me.

Wife   They might. She might. And you might as well try. We've got nothing to lose.

*The **Poor Man** walks into the forest as the **Villagers** speak.*

Villager 1   So he left the village and went into the forest–

Villager 2   Into the darkest centre of the forest–

Villager 1   Where no light shone and the shadows were thick.

Villager 2   Where no birds sang and the silence was deep.

Villager 1   And there, in the very centre of the forest, he prayed.

*The **Poor Man** prays.*

Poor Man   O, Durga, great goddess. Hear my prayer. I'm starving. My family is starving. If we don't eat soon, we'll all die! Hear me, Durga. You're my last hope.

***Durga** enters carrying a pot, as the **Villagers** speak.*

Villager 1   And as his words faded, a light began to glow.

Villager 2   A light in the dark, shining brighter and brighter.

Villager 1   A great golden shaft of brilliant light–

Villager 2   Streaming from heaven down to earth.

Villager 1   And there, in the light, was the goddess herself.

*The **Poor Man** looks up and sees **Durga**.*

Poor Man   Durga? Is it really you?

Durga   Yes. I am Durga, and I've heard your prayer. You're a good man, and your wife's a good woman. I'll see that you go hungry no more. Here, take this.

Durga gives him the pot.

Poor Man   It's a pot.

Durga   That's right. A pot.

Poor Man   A cooking pot.

Durga   Quite so. It is a cooking pot.

*The **Poor Man** looks into the pot.*

Poor Man   It's a very beautiful cooking pot.

Durga   Indeed, it is beautiful.

Poor Man   But … it's empty.

Durga   That's right. It's empty.

Poor Man   May I say something, O great Durga?

Durga   You may.

Poor Man   It is a beautiful pot – but what we really need
is something to put in it.

Durga   Do as I tell you, and the pot shall soon be full.
First, turn the pot over.

He turns the pot over.

Durga   Now tap it three times.

He taps it three times.

Durga   And now turn it back.

He turns it back.

Villager 1   And when he'd done what she said–

Villager 2   The smell that arose–

Villager 1   The delicious aroma that tickled his nose–

Villager 2   Was so–

Poor Man   Mouth-watering …

Villager 1   And the food that he saw cooking in the pot was so–

Poor Man   Appetizing …

Villager 2   That he just had to eat it straight away.

The Poor Man eats from the pot.

Durga   Have you eaten your fill?

Poor Man   Yes – for now.

Durga   Good. Each time you do this, the pot will cook. Take it, with my blessing, and be hungry no more.

Durga goes. The Poor Man takes the pot to his Wife as the Villagers speak.

Villager 1 And the goddess was gone.

Villager 2 And so was he.

Villager 1 Straight back to his wife.

Villager 2 And he told her what had happened, and showed her the pot.

*The **Poor Man** gives the pot to his **Wife**.*

Poor Man Turn it over, and tap it three times.

She does so.

Poor Man Now turn it back.

She does so.

Poor Man And look! It's full of food, and you can eat your fill.

Wife   Thanks. I will!

She eats.

Wife   Well? And was I right to send you into the forest?

Poor Man   Yes, my love, you were.

Wife   I know I was. The great goddess heard your prayer and smiled on us, and now we'll never go hungry again.

*The **Poor Man** and his **Wife** go.*

Villager 1   They would never have gone hungry again.

Villager 2   And everything would have been all right for the rest of their lives.

Villager 1   Except that word got around.

*A **Gossip** enters and speaks to the audience.*

Gossip   Have you heard about that cooking pot?

Villager 1 And the word went around.

Gossip It's a magic pot!

Villager 2 From mouth to mouth.

Gossip It cooks food whenever you want.

Villager 1 From door to door.

Gossip One minute it's empty, and the next, it's full!

Villager 2 It went all around the village.

Gossip It tastes delicious. I know, because I've had some.

Villager 1 From house to house, from ear to ear.

Gossip And they say it was a gift from the goddess herself.

Villager 2 Until it came to the house and the ear of the rich man.

*The **Rich Man** enters and speaks to the **Gossip**.*

Rich Man   A magic pot?

Gossip   Yes, that's right.

Rich Man   That cooks by itself?

Gossip   Yes, that's right.

Rich Man   A gift from Durga?

Gossip   Yes, that's right.

Rich Man   It's outrageous! A disgrace! It's just not fair!

The **Gossip** *goes.*

Villager 1   And he was very angry.

Villager 2   Because you know what they say.

Villager 1   Those who have, always want more.

Villager 2   And he was determined to have that pot.

Rich Man   *(To himself)* Why should they have a magic pot? They are the poorest people in the village. They don't deserve a gift from the goddess. A gift from the goddess should go to someone like me. It's all wrong. There's been a dreadful mistake. That pot belongs to me. I'll make sure that it's mine.

Villager 1   As you can see, he was determined to have it.

Villager 2   And he thought long and hard about how he should get it.

Villager 1   He couldn't just take it – that would be stealing.

Villager 2   And even *he* couldn't just steal things.

Villager 1   He had to think of some plan, some plot.

Villager 2   Some way of getting hold of the magic pot.

Villager 1   And it wasn't long before he'd thought of it.

Rich Man   That's it! I've got it! That's the way I'll do it!

Villager 2   And he called his daughter and spoke to her.

*The rich man's **Daughter** enters.*

Rich Man   Listen, my dear. I've been thinking.

Daughter   Yes, Father.

Rich Man   It's about time you got married.

Daughter   Married?

Rich Man   That's right, yes. Married.

Daughter   But I don't want to get married.

Rich Man   Nonsense. Of course you do. You've been at home far too long.

Daughter   But I haven't seen anyone I want to marry.

Rich Man   You haven't looked hard enough.

Daughter   Father–

Rich Man   Daughter! I have decided! You are going to be married. And you will have a grand wedding feast. The grandest the village has ever seen. Everyone will be invited. And everyone will bring a gift.

*The **Rich Man** and his **Daughter** go. The **Villagers** remain on stage.*

Scene 2

The **Rich Man** enters with his **Daughter** and
her **Husband**. They stand together, proudly, as
if they are at the wedding feast. The **Villagers**
speak.

Villager 1   And so she was married.

Villager 2   And it was a grand occasion.

Villager 1   No expense was spared.

Villager 2   The whole village was invited to the feast.

Villager 1   And everyone brought a gift for the bride.

Villager 2   As tradition said they should.

Villager 1   One brought a goat.

Villager 2   One brought a loaf of bread.

Villager 1   One brought a scarf, and a bracelet.

Villager 2   One brought a basket of eggs.

Villager 1   Everyone brought something.

Villager 2   Everyone, except for–

*The **Poor Man** and his **Wife** enter.*

*The **Villagers**, the **Rich Man**, his **Daughter**
and her **Husband** turn and point at them.
They speak together.*

All Them!

*The **Poor Man** and his **Wife** speak together.*

Man/Wife Us?

Rich Man That's right! How dare you come here without
a gift!

Villagers Without a gift!

Daughter How dare you come to my wedding and bring
nothing!

Villagers	Bring nothing!
Rich Man	It's disgraceful!
Villagers	Disgraceful!
Daughter	Outrageous!
Villagers	Outrageous!
Rich Man	Shameful!
Villagers	Shameful!
Wife	But we have nothing.
Poor Man	We're poor.
Wife	We don't have anything to give.
Rich Man	Nothing? Are you sure about that?
Poor Man	Yes, we're sure. We have nothing.
Rich Man	Not even a pot?

Wife   What?

Rich Man   You don't even have a cooking pot? Everyone has a cooking pot. Even if they don't have anything to put in it.

Poor Man   Well, as a matter of fact we do. But–

Rich Man   But what?

Wife   It's a special pot.

Rich Man   Then if it's special, that's all the more reason to give it to my daughter. As a mark of your respect, and gratitude for being invited to her wedding.

Daughter   Exactly.

Poor Man   But–

Rich Man   No excuses! Go and bring that pot here now. If you don't, you'll be cast out of the village.

Villagers   Cast out!

Rich Man   I am the head man, and you'll do as I say.

*The **Poor Man** and his **Wife** look at each other. Then they shrug and walk across to the pot. The **Poor Man** picks it up, and they go back to the **Rich Man** as the **Villagers** speak.*

Villager 1   So that's what they did.

Villager 2   What else could they do?

Villager 1   It was tradition.

Villager 2   And they couldn't go against tradition.

Villager 1   The village was their only home.

Villager 2   And they couldn't be turned out of their only home.

Villager 1   Not even for a magic pot.

Villager 2   Not even for a pot given by the great goddess Durga.

Villager 1   So they went home and fetched it.

Villager 2   And gave it away.

*The **Poor Man** gives the pot to the rich man's **Daughter**.*

Daughter   Thank you.

*The **Rich Man** takes the pot from his **Daughter**.*

Rich Man   Thank *you*!

*His **Daughter** stares at him, shocked. The **Rich Man** speaks to the **Poor Man** and his **Wife**.*

Rich Man   Don't just stand there. What are you waiting for? The wedding feast is over. You can go back home.

*He speaks to his **Daughter**.*

Rich Man   And you! Go back to your home with your new husband.

*The **Rich Man** turns and goes, with the pot. His **Daughter** stares after him for a moment. She is angry. Then she goes with her **Husband**.*

Poor Man   He tricked us!

Wife   That's right.

Poor Man   He knew about the pot!

Wife   Of course he knew.

Poor Man   But how did he know?

Wife   Everyone in the village knew.

Poor Man   He invited us to the wedding just so he could take the pot.

Wife   And we were silly enough to go.

Poor Man   Now we've got nothing! We've got less than nothing. We'll starve again. And there's nothing we can do.

Wife   Actually there is.

Poor Man   What?

Wife   There is something we can do.

Poor Man   What can we do?

Wife   At least, there's something you can do.

Poor Man   Me? What can I do?

Wife   The same as you did before. You can go back into the forest. You can pray to Durga. Tell her what happened and ask her for another pot.

Poor Man   You can't be serious!

Wife   I'm very serious.

Poor Man   Go back a second time?

Wife Yes.

Poor Man Ask Durga again?

Wife That's right.

Poor Man She won't listen to me.

Wife Then you'll have lost nothing.

Poor Man She might be angry with me. She might blast me to bits!

Wife Then you won't be starving any more. Your suffering will be over.

Poor Man I can't!

Wife You must!

Poor Man I won't!

Wife You will!

*The poor man's **Wife** turns from him and goes.*

Scene 3

*The **Poor Man** walks to the centre of the stage as the **Villagers** speak. He kneels as if he is in the forest, praying to Durga.*

Villager 1   And he did. He went back into the forest.

Villager 2   Back into that darkest centre of the forest.

Villager 1   Where no birds sang and the silence was deep.

Villager 2   And there, in the very centre of the forest, once more, he prayed.

Villager 1   And the forest was filled with light.

Villager 2   And there, in the light, was the goddess.

Durga enters carrying a second pot. The Poor Man looks up and sees her.

Durga   You again.

Poor Man   Yes, great goddess. Me again.

Durga   What do you want this time? Have you come to tell me how wonderful my gift is?

Poor Man   That's right, Durga. It is a most wonderful gift.

Durga   And to thank me for it?

Poor Man   I do thank you, from the bottom of my heart.

Durga   And to tell me that you've lost it?

Poor Man   Yes, Durga, it's true. I have lost it.

Durga   Or, to be more correct, you gave it away.

Poor Man   Yes, I did. I gave it away. But I couldn't help it—

Durga Don't say anymore! I know what happened. I know all that happens. I am a goddess, remember.

Poor Man A most great, and powerful … and merciful goddess.

Durga Am I? Am I merciful?

Poor Man I believe so, Durga.

Durga You mean your wife believes so.

Poor Man Yes – but so do I–

Durga Merciful enough to give you a second pot? That's what you've come for, isn't it?

Poor Man It was my wife's idea.

Durga Do you want a second pot?

Poor Man Yes.

She holds out the pot.

Durga   Here, then. Take this.

Poor Man   O great Durga …

Durga   Say nothing! Just take the pot, and go.

*The **Poor Man** gets up and takes the pot.*

Poor Man   Is it the same as the first one? Does it work in the same way?

Durga   The same – more or less. And look after this one. I do not wish to be troubled again.

Poor Man   No, great goddess. I promise. You won't be.

Durga goes.

Villager 1 Straight away he went running back home through the forest.

Villager 2 He burst into his house and showed his wife the new pot.

*The **Poor Man** calls out.*

Poor Man Wife! Wife! See what Durga has given us!

*The **Wife** enters.*

Wife You see? You should have more faith in the gods.

Poor Man You're right, I should – and more faith in you.

Wife I'm glad you think so. Does this pot work in the same way as the first?

Poor Man That's what the goddess said. The same way – more or less.

Wife More or less? I wonder what she meant by that?

Poor Man   Nothing. Or perhaps the food it cooks is even tastier than the first.

Wife   There's only one way to find out. Let's turn it over and give it a tap.

*She takes the pot from the **Poor Man**. She turns it over, taps it three times, and turns it back again. She looks inside.*

Poor Man   Well?

Wife   I don't believe it.

Poor Man   What?

Wife   Nothing.

Poor Man   What!

Wife   There's nothing in there. Nothing at all.

Poor Man   Let me see.

*The **Poor Man** looks inside the pot. Then he looks at his **Wife**.*

Poor Man   You're right. Nothing. Absolutely nothing.

*The **Poor Man** and his **Wife** stare into the pot. The **Villagers** speak. As they do, the faces of the **Poor Man** and his **Wife** grow more and more frightened. They can see something horrible inside the pot.*

Villager 1   Nothing doing.

Villager 2   Nothing cooking.

Villager 1   But the pot wasn't exactly empty.

Villager 2   Because, as they stared into it–

Villager 1   As they looked into its dark depths–

Villager 2   Something appeared out of those dark depths.

Villager 1   Something terrible–

Villager 2   Something horrible–

Villager 1   Rushing up towards them out of those dark depths–

Villager 2   And bursting upon them with smoke and fire!

*The **Poor Man** and his **Wife** jump back from the pot in terror. A **Demon**, carrying a club, enters and stands before them. The **Villagers** and the **Poor Man** and his **Wife** all cry out.*

All   A demon!

*The **Demon** roars and wields the club.*

Villager 1   With a club–

Villager 2   And this terrible demon–

Villager 1   Beat the poor man–

Villager 2   From head to toe.

*The **Demon** beats the **Poor Man** with the club.*
*The **Poor Man** cries out.*

Poor Man   No! Ow! Stop! Please! Help! It hurts! Ah!

*The **Demon** stops beating the **Poor Man** and goes.*

Villager 1   How the poor man groaned.

Villager 2   How the poor man moaned.

Villager 1   How the poor man wailed.

Villager 2   How the poor man wept.

Villager 1   How he cried and wailed and sobbed and throbbed.

Villager 2   And how his poor wife laughed and laughed.

*The poor man's **Wife** laughs.*

Poor Man   What are you laughing at? It's not funny! I've just been beaten all over my body. I'm bruised all over, and all you can do is laugh as if it's some kind of joke. Stop it! It's not a joke! Stop laughing!

Wife   I'm sorry. I'm not laughing at you. I'm laughing at the marvellous thought I've just had.

Poor Man   What thought?

Wife   It's so marvellous, I can't tell you. But don't worry. You'll soon find out.

*The rich man's **Daughter** enters. The poor man's **Wife** goes across to her. The two talk together quietly as the **Villagers** speak.*

Villager 1   Then his wife went to the house of the rich man's daughter.

Villager 2	And she spoke to the daughter, and the daughter listened.
Villager 1	As she listened, a smile spread across her face.
Villager 2	And when the poor man's wife had finished, the rich man's daughter said:
Daughter	Yes! I think that's a wonderful idea!

*The poor man's **Wife** goes back to her husband and speaks to him.*

Wife	There, now. That's done. We'll soon have our pot back.
Poor Man	How do you know?
Wife	Trust me. I know.

*The **Rich Man** enters with the first pot. His **Daughter** goes to him and they talk together quietly as the **Villagers** speak.*

Villager 1	Then the rich man's daughter went to her father's house.

Villager 2 And told her father about the second pot.

Villager 1 But she didn't tell him everything.

*The **Rich Man** speaks to his **Daughter**.*

Rich Man A second pot?

Daughter That's right, Father. A second pot.

Rich Man Better than the first?

Daughter That's what they're saying. Much, much better. And you should hear the way they boast about it. You should hear the way they laugh at you–

Rich Man Laugh at me?

Daughter Because the pot you've got is only second best.

Rich Man Second best, is it? Do they know who I am? I'm the most important man in the village. I don't have second best of anything!

Daughter That's what they're saying.

Rich Man   We'll soon see about that. I've got to have that second pot. I'm going to have that second pot!

Daughter   But how? You can't take it from them. That would be stealing.

Rich Man   That's true. What can I do, then? How can I get that pot?

Daughter   Go and see them. Take the first pot. Offer to give it back to them in exchange for the second.

Rich Man   What if they refuse?

Daughter   How can they refuse? You're the head man, aren't you? And if they are difficult, just shout at them. You're good at that.

Rich Man   You're right! I am the head man. They'll have to do what I want. I'll go and see them straight away.

*The **Daughter** goes. The **Rich Man** goes across to the **Poor Man** and his **Wife** as the **Villagers** speak.*

Villager 2   So off he went to the home of the poor man and his wife–

Villager 1   Taking the magic pot with him.

Villager 2   And the rich man told the poor man and his wife he wanted to give the pot back to them.

*The **Poor Man** speaks to the **Rich Man**.*

Poor Man   Give it back to us?

Rich Man   Yes, that's right.

Poor Man   That's very kind of you.

Rich Man   Yes, I know. I can be kind when I want to.

Wife   It is kind of you. Thank you for your offer, but we don't need that pot now. We have a second one.

Rich Man   I know you do. I've heard all about it – a most marvellous pot.

Poor Man   Marvellous? I wouldn't say that–

*His **Wife** interrupts him.*

Wife   Yes, indeed it is, most marvellous.

Rich Man   But this first pot – the one you most generously gave to my daughter – and which she most generously gave to me – this pot is also marvellous.

Wife   That's true. It is.

Rich Man   Then I'm sure you wouldn't mind swapping them. I will give you this marvellous pot, and you can give me that one.

Poor Man   You want to swap them? But–

*The poor man's **Wife** interrupts him again.*

Wife   We'd be very happy to swap them.

Rich Man   Good–

Wife   But I have to tell you the truth. If we do swap them, you'll be getting the worst of the bargain.

Rich Man   In what way?

Wife   This second pot is not as marvellous as the first.

Rich Man   Indeed? That's not what I've heard. I've heard that the second pot is much more marvellous than the first.

Wife   I'm afraid you've heard wrong. It isn't.

Poor Man   It certainly isn't.

Rich Man   I think it is.

Wife   You can think what you like, but I'm telling you, it isn't. You'll be better off keeping the first pot, and leaving us with this one.

*The **Rich Man** shouts angrily.*

Rich Man   I won't have this! I know what you're up to! You're just pretending it's not as good so you can keep it! You can't fool me! I'm the head man! Show me how the second pot works! Here and now!

Wife You want us to make this pot work?

Rich Man Yes!

Wife Did you hear that, husband?

Poor Man I heard.

Wife Go on, then. Make it work.

Poor Man I can't.

Rich Man Can't? What do you mean, you can't?

Poor Man I mean ... I'm scared.

Rich Man Scared? What is there to be scared of?

Poor Man The thing that comes out of that pot.

Rich Man This is just another trick. You're pretending there's something to be scared of. You'll be telling me next there's a demon or something in there!

Poor Man There is–

| Rich Man | That's enough! No more of these lies. If you won't make the pot work, I will. Give it to me. |

*The **Rich Man** puts the first pot down and picks up the second.*

| Rich Man | Does it work in the same way? |

| Wife | Yes. In exactly the same way. |

| Rich Man | Very well. Now we'll see. |

*The **Rich Man** turns the pot over, taps it three times, and turns it back. He looks inside.*

Rich Man Nothing!

Wife Are you sure?

Rich Man Completely sure. There's nothing.

Wife It takes a while to work. Keep looking.

*The **Rich Man** looks inside again.*

Rich Man I tell you, I can't see anything cooking.

*The **Demon** enters behind him, carrying a club.*

Wife Oh, but there is, and I'll give you a clue. The thing that's cooking smells like you!

*The **Demon** taps the **Rich Man**. The **Rich Man** turns, sees the **Demon**, and cries out. The **Demon** roars and beats the **Rich Man**.*

Villager 1   And he tripped him up.

Villager 2   And knocked him down.

Villager 1   He beat that rich man–

Villager 2   All over the town.

Villager 1   And we came out to watch.

Villager 2   And we lined the streets.

Villager 1   As he cracked his head.

Villager 2   And stamped on his feet.

Villager 1   And the air was filled–

Villager 2   With hooting and laughter.

Villager 1   As the rich man ran–

Villager 2   And the beast followed after–

Villager 1   Over the hills and far away.

Villager 2   And he's not been seen again from that day.

*The **Rich Man** runs off, followed by the **Demon**. The **Poor Man** turns to his **Wife**.*

Poor Man   You planned all that to happen. You tricked him, even better than he tricked us.

Wife   I had a little help from his daughter.

Poor Man   His daughter helped you?

Wife   She knew how greedy and selfish her father was. She was only too glad to get rid of him.

Poor Man   But it was your idea.

Wife Yes, it was.

Poor Man Wife – you're a genius.

Wife I wouldn't say that. I just have some common sense – and faith in the gods. It's Durga we must thank. She sent us the second pot as a way of getting the first one back.

Poor Man I can see that now. And of course we shall always be grateful to Durga. But I still say you're a genius.

Wife All right. If you insist.

*The **Poor Man** picks up the first pot.*

Poor Man Thanks to you – and to Durga – we have our pot back. Now we'll never go hungry.

Wife And not just us, because this pot doesn't just belong to us. It belongs to the whole village. Everyone can have their share of it.

Villager 1 And that's the story of how in our village–

Villager 2   Our little village in India–

Villager 1   Something marvellous happened.

Villager 2   How a poor man and a rich man changed places.

Villager 1   How we received a gift from heaven.

Villager 2   How none of us ever went hungry again.

Villager 1   And how we lost our head man.

Villager 2   And gained – a head woman.

Poor Man   And quite right too.

They all go.

The End